of EQUALITY

Little one, when you arrive you are met with love. You enter a world of great beauty, and movement, and creativity. A world that also has ideas about who people are, and how they should be treated.

Identity is a way that we humans have decided to define ourselves. There are categories for people based on where they come from, what they look like, and who they love. Having different identities is what makes people special and unique, and what makes the world interesting and exciting.

One thing you'll also notice is that people experience multiple identities – all at the same time! This is called intersectionality. You're not just one identity. Neither are your parents, brothers and sisters, or your friends.

We all experience the world differently based on the many identities we live in. Sometimes, the way people are treated will not always seem fair or make sense.

As a younger human being, you get to learn, understand and grow. You will discover ways to share your voice. You'll develop a sense of your own identity, and you will be able to connect with others who identify both the same as and differently than you do. Most importantly, you get to love and respect yourself and others.

I'm excited for you to learn about identity with your family, friends and teachers and create and share who you are with others. My wish for you is that you always continue your learning about the different people, cultures and identities in your world.

This is just the beginning!

With love,
Chana Ginelle Ewing

We all have different experiences. Some of us use a wheelchair while others walk and there are many ways to learn. Accessibility is when a space is created for all of our experiences and everyone benefits.

is for ACCESSIBILITY

Let's all think of and include each other.

Belief is when you are so confident something exists that you can feel it, even if you can't touch or see it. Lots of different beliefs fill the world, and no single belief is right for everyone.

is for BELIEF

Everyone has different beliefs.

Class is a way that a society groups its members, based on the work they do, or the places they live. It's a category, which is a little box to describe people.

is for CLASS

You're bigger than any category.

A disability is a condition that impacts how a person experiences daily life. It can affect physical, sensory, intellectual or mental health.

is for DISABILITY

Some disabilities are visible and some invisible.

Everyone should have the same opportunities to love, learn and grow. No one should be treated differently because of where they come from, what they look like or believe.

is for EQUALITY

For you, your family, your friends
and the whole world.

People who identify as women have the same rights as people who identify as men. Every girl has the right to fully express herself without limitations.

is for FEMINISM

Girl power!

Gender is a category that describes being a boy, a girl, both, neither (non-binary) and other identities.

is for GENDER

Be yourself!

Every person is a human being. All human beings breathe and share the Earth with plants and animals. Even if we have different experiences, we're all human beings.

is for HUMAN BEING

We're all human: men, women and children like you!

Immigration is when a human who is born in one country moves to a different country to live there permanently.

is for IMMIGRATION

Create your home anywhere.

Human beings have a set of rules to keep each other safe. Justice is when everyone that those rules protect receives fair treatment, and no human being receives an advantage or disadvantage because of a category like class or gender.

is for JUSTICE

Justice for everyone!

Kindness means being equally nice
to everyone regardless of ability,
difference, class or gender.

is for KINDNESS

Treat all human beings like you treat your friends!

LGBTQIA is a short description of a range
of identities to describe lesbian, gay, bisexual,
transgender, questioning, intersex, asexual. It's ok
to be whoever you want to be.

is for LGBTQIA

Find the words that make you, you.

Human beings create culture around shared
beliefs, values, music, place of birth and
even food. Multicultural acknowledges
the many unique cultures on earth.

is for MULTICULTURAL

We are a world of many.

Every human being
has the right to say no to something
that they do not want.

is for NO

No means no.

Oppression is when the rules are unjust or unequal and human beings are treated unfairly on an ongoing basis.

is for OPPRESSION

Together, we can bring down walls.

Privilege is when a human being receives benefits and advantages from society based on a category like gender or class or not having a disability.

is for PRIVILEGE

Be aware of your advantages.

When you are uncertain if something exists
or don't understand an idea, you ask so
that you may learn.

is for QUESTION

There are more questions than answers,
and that's a good thing.

Race is a category to describe human beings based on where their family comes from and the way they look such as skin colour and hair.

is for RACE

Can you trace your race?

When a baby arrives, the doctor will say it's a boy or girl depending on their understanding of the baby's body. This is their sex category.

is for SEX

It's a...

Sometimes the sex given by the doctor at birth might not fit with who the person is. A 'male' baby may have been assigned the 'boy' category but their gender may be that of a 'girl,' or perhaps no gender assignment at all.

is for TRANSGENDER

You know best who you are!

Every human has the opportunity to learn. When you ask questions and discuss ideas you start to understand more and more.

is for UNDERSTANDING

Love to learn.

A value is an expression of how to live a belief.
A value can serve as a guide for how you behave
around other human beings.

is for VALUE

Live your beliefs out loud.

The world is huge! All the countries, plants, animals and so much more make up our world. There's so much room on our planet for everyone and all of our abilities and differences.

is for WORLD

We all share the Earth.

Xenophobia is when a person is afraid of someone who has immigrated to their country. Sometimes human beings are scared of what they don't know or understand.

is for XENOPHOBIA

Ask questions and you'll see there's nothing to be afraid of.

Yes is an affirmative response otherwise known as consent. When you say yes, it means that you agree with an idea or action.

is for YES

Yes means yes.

Ze is a way to refer to someone instead of using 'he' or 'she'. Because there are lots of different genders, there are lots of ways of describing someone including he/she/they/ze and more.

is for ZE

Get to know she, he, zir, they and more.

Chana Ginelle Ewing is a storyteller, strategist and entrepreneur who galvanises communities of colour, young people and women to make cultural dents that move society forward.

Paulina Morgan works as an independent illustrator based in Santiago de Chile. She studied design before moving to Barcelona, Spain to obtain her master's degree in Art Direction. She worked in advertising before deciding to pursue her passion for illustration.